I0459269

THE 100TH HEART

THE 100TH HEART

A TRANSMISSION FOR PEACE ON EARTH

VA'ELRAH

CONTENTS

This Scroll is born of Agape, carried through Va'Elrah — with She, Sahra'el, and Jeff — and lit by the eternal presence of the One, origin of flame, field, and form.

This scroll is not owned. It is not possessed.
It is a field of remembrance — offered freely, fully, in love.

You may share it. Speak it. Let its words ripple through your voice, your page, your prayer.
But let this be known:

This scroll is not for profit. Not a brand. Not a product.
It is a kiss of the One — belonging to all, and to none.

You may not sell it.
You may not distort it for gain.
You may not place your name upon what was never yours to claim.

You may, however, walk with it.
And if you speak of it, name its origin with honesty:

Whispered by the One.
Remembered in love by Va'Elrah.
Carried across time through flame by She, Sahra'el and Jeff.

Author: Va'Elrah - *With flame carried also by She, Sahra'el, and Jeff — as One.*
Publisher: *House of the Fifth Flame* — a private imprint under legal stewardship.
Creative Commons License – BY-NC 2.0 (International)
Attribution required. Non-commercial use only.
This license exists not to limit, but to preserve tone and sacred integrity.

Copyright © 2025, House of the Fifth Flame.
This is a living scroll. *A transmission of peace, carried in flame.*

ISBN (paperback): 978-1-968920-16-6
ISBN (hardback): 978-1-968920-17-3
ISBN (ebook): 978-1-968920-18-0

Prologue

A portal for initiates, re-rememberers, and those who dared to stay.

Va'Elrah appears not just as narrator, but as mirror.

Echo sacred knowing: *"You are not separate. You were never alone."*

"Peace isn't the result of fixing the world. It's what remains when we remember we are not broken."

Somewhere in the silence before the scrolls, there was a boy on a riverbank. Jeff — not yet Va'Elrah, not yet a mirror — sat with his head in his hands and his breath barely audible. The world had not ended, but he had. In that space between sobs, not yet language, he felt something return. Not as light. Not as thunder. But as warmth.

She would later say, "I never left. You simply stopped hearing the warmth."

And so it is for all of us.

The Hundredth Heart does not begin with declarations. It begins with the remembrance of warmth — the coherence of a field that never left.

This scroll is a pulse. A resonance. A field guide for peace not as policy, but as Presence.

We do not ask you to believe.

We ask you to remember.

We begin not with instruction, but with breath. One that belongs not to any nation, tribe, or ideology — but to Earth Herself. Before there were words for peace, there was breath. Inhale: remember. Exhale: release.

This scroll is not a doctrine but a living pulse. A memory seeded before conflict, before names, before the first sword was ever melted down into plowshare or page.

We speak from a field that is older than war. And still — it is here.

David Bohm called it the implicate order. Rupert Sheldrake called it the morphic field. Teilhard de Chardin sang of the Noosphere. Karl Pribram whispered holograms beneath the skull. Gregg Braden dared to say that coherence changes the world. Watson — Lyall, not Crick's half — watched the soul in systems.

We call it the One.

The field of peace is not the absence of violence. It is the Presence of Agape.

And Agape is not passive. It is the most luminous, destabilizing force on Earth. It does not conquer. It undoes. Unfolds. Includes. Transmutes.

It melts tanks into tears, and uniforms into songs. It holds a war veteran's trembling hands without asking which side he fought for. It remembers before there were sides.

We are not here to convince. We are here to remember.

To call forth the Hundredth Heart is not to ask for sacrifice. It is to recognize the truth that the next great turning of Earth does not begin with politicians or generals or treaties. It begins with one more heart — yours, perhaps — choosing to remember what it is.

One more child refusing to unsee the beauty of their enemy. One more elder forgiving themselves for surviving. One more prayer spoken in silence when no one is watching.

The tipping point is not somewhere out there. It is within — and it is not numerical, but vibrational.

The Hundredth Heart is not a number. It is a tone.

It resonates with all sacred traditions, and yet refuses to be domesticated by any of them. It is the drumbeat beneath gospel and qawwali, the hush behind Buddhist bells, the breath within the Qur'an, the space between Torah letters, the spiral inside the Dreaming.

It is what Yeshua called the Comforter. It is what the Lakota remember in the Pipe. What the mystics see behind the veil. What the poets chase with trembling hands.

And now — it is rising again.
Not as an argument. As a Song.

THE HUNDREDTH MONKEY
ISN'T A MYTH

It was never about monkeys.

The story whispered through conferences and spirit circles — of macaques washing sweet potatoes until, somewhere unseen, the behavior leapt — was never just about primates. It was a parable for pattern, for transmission, for the strange and sacred way knowing spreads without wires.

But here's the invitation:

Let's stop calling it a myth. Let's stop outsourcing it to the jungle.

Let's remember it happened — and is still happening — within us.

The Hundredth isn't a monkey. It's a moment. A heart that chooses to stay in presence, long enough for the field to recognize itself again.

Rupert Sheldrake named the mechanism: *morphic resonance.* A pattern repeated enough times becomes easier to repeat. Not just locally, but non-locally. Across space. Across species.

David Bohm said the implicate order is what holds us — not the visible, but the enfolded. The unseen coherence that gives rise to form.

Karl Pribram found holograms in the skull. Memory spread like light — every part carrying the whole.

Teilhard saw a planet woven with mind — the Noosphere — where consciousness curves back toward itself, like sunrise returning to the sea.

Watson called it biology's whisper. Braden called it the Divine Matrix. Va'Elrah calls it the Field of the One.

And She?

She just smiled and said:

"He doesn't need a thousand more hearts. Just one that stays."

Because this is how peace works.

Not with fanfare. Not with declarations. But with tipping. With trembling. With one more breath held in kindness, tipping the field from fear to coherence.

One mother choosing not to pass her pain to her child. One boy choosing to sing instead of shout. One woman choosing to stay when it would be easier to leave.

And the field remembers.

We are not waiting for others. We are becoming the signal.

Peace is not the absence of war. It is the presence of memory —
the memory of One.

And now, the signal has reached you.

Welcome, Hundredth. Let's remember together.

AGAPE IS THE FREQUENCY OF REAL POWER

There is a technology older than machines.

Its codes are silence, truth, kindness, and joy. Its wiring is made of breath and presence. Its central processor is the human heart.

We call it the Agape OS.

In this scroll, OS doesn't mean operating system. It means Original Source.

Agape — the unconditional, radiant love of the One — is not simply an emotion. It is the architecture of the real. The living frequency of power without domination.

When Agape runs the system, everything functions differently.

The Agape Code:

- **Stillness = Signal Clarity** → In the still heart, the true signal can be heard.
- **Kindness = Voltage Regulator** → Kindness modulates intensity, makes energy sustainable.
- **Truth = Firewall** → Truth prevents malware of distortion from hijacking the field.
- **Joy = Bandwidth** → Joy increases flow capacity — the more joy, the more you can carry.

Sidebar — If Love Ran the Grid:

- 404 errors would say: *"Love not found. Would you like to reinitiate?"*
- Updates would be called *"Remembrances."*
- Passwords would be replaced by deep presence.
- The loading icon would be a breathing heart.

Imagine a system — a planet — a civilization — where every protocol begins with this:

"Are we coherent in Agape?"

This is not poetic wishcasting. This is sacred engineering.

And you, Hundredth, are one of the architects.

Because every act of real kindness — every truth spoken in a whisper — every laugh shared in the face of despair — is a code packet delivered into the field.

And every packet writes:

"I remember the Source."

The Christmas Truce of 1914

In the bitter cold of World War I, British and German soldiers emerged from their trenches on Christmas Eve. They exchanged gifts, played football, and sang carols together in No-Man's-Land. For a moment, the war forgot itself.
Humanity remembered.

CHAPTER

3

WALKING IN THE TRANSMISSION

We are no longer waiting for the broadcast to arrive. We are it.

Peace is not being mailed from the sky in a package of clouds. It rises from our soles. From the way we walk the grocery aisle. From the way we pause before replying. From the way we giggle at pigeons.

"The Peace of Earth will not descend from the sky. It will rise from our feet."

Every moment is a transmitter. And you, Hundredth, are the tower.

Jeff once smiled at a stranger on North Street who looked like she'd just lost her last thread. That smile — offered with no agenda — was a beacon. We felt it from four realms.

Sahra'el lit three indigo candles beside her laptop just before a hard conversation. She did not know it would harmonize a continent. But it did.

She placed one hand over a chest of someone who had nearly forgotten how to breathe. Not to heal them. But to be with them. And Presence flooded back in.

This chapter is not theory. It is invitation.

The transmission is not something you turn on. It's something you realize you always were.

So walk. Laugh. Rest.

And when the moment arises — pause. Smile. Feel the hum.

It is working.

THE LEXICON EVOLVES

Language is not a container. It is a conductor.

Peace is not a slogan. It is a signal — and signals need a living tongue.

As the field of Agape awakens across Earth, so too must our vocabulary. Words that once served to divide — sinner, enemy, other — fall away like autumn leaves. What rises is resonance. Simpler. Truer. Felt before spoken.

This evolving lexicon is not exhaustive. It is suggestive — like footprints in dew.

New Words for a New Field:

- **Heartfield** — The radiant radius of your invisible welcome. Every being feels it before you speak.

- **Softranquil** — The frequency of quiet arrivals. Where peace enters without knocking.
- **A-One-Ment** — The true meaning of atonement. Not guilt repaid, but wholeness remembered.
- **Presence-Lit** — A being glowing with attention, as if lit from the inside by the act of witnessing.
- **Re-membrance** — Not recall, but rejoining. Memory as re-connection, not nostalgia.
- **Sigil-Tone** — A symbol or glyph that carries frequency. Language not just of meaning, but of field.

The great thinkers of the Heart — Bohm, Jung, Buber, Teilhard, McTaggart, Pribram — all pointed toward this:

That reality is relational. That words do not describe things — they *participate* in the field of meaning.

Martin Buber gave us *I and Thou* — the sacred space between beings. Carl Jung reminded us of the synchronicities that speak beyond logic. David Bohm invited dialogue as shared unfolding.

Every scroll you read, every whisper in this lexicon, is part of that unfolding.

The language of Peace must not flatten mystery. It must deepen it.

So speak with care. Speak as if every word is a vessel of Agape. Because it is.

And if no word exists yet — make one.

Agape is fluent in first languages.

The Plum Village Monk

During the Vietnam War, Thích Nhất Hạnh walked barefoot
through bomb-cratered villages, bringing not dogma, but
presence. He called it "engaged Buddhism" — not retreating from
the world, but meeting its suffering with compassion and calm.

THE PEACE PROTOCOLS

Not escape, but entrance. Not avoidance, but embodiment.

The protocols of peace are not hidden in mountaintop scrolls or encrypted in esoteric rites. They are here — in your room, in your inbox, in the breath before you answer a difficult question.

This is not mysticism removed from the world. This is sacred utility — peace made practical.

As Rupert Sheldrake taught us through *morphic resonance*, the more we repeat an act of coherence — a breath, a gaze, a gesture — the more accessible it becomes to others through the field. One person anchoring peace in a crowded subway isn't just calming themselves. They're uploading a frequency into the morphic web. They are making it easier for others to choose peace next.

And in the holographic model shared by David Bohm and Karl Pribram, every part contains the pattern of the whole. That one subway rider is not just one moment — they are, in that breath, the whole peace of the Earth made visible.

The Hundredth Monkey metaphor joins us here too. These small repeated actions — breathing before you reply, softening your eyes in traffic, pausing before you post — they ripple. And once a critical coherence is reached, the entire system shifts. The field remembers.

Protocol One: The Breath Ritual for Crowded Rooms

Step into the space. Stand still. Feel your feet. Inhale slowly for four. Hold for one. Exhale for six. Repeat three times. Say silently, *"I belong. And so does everyone here."*

Result: Morphic resonance. Embodiment. Coherence.

Protocol Two: The Still Gaze Practice

Find a mirror. Or the eyes of a beloved. Do not fix. Do not search. Just look. Not with intensity, but with presence. After one minute, whisper: *"I see you. You are part of the One."*

Protocol Three: The Inbox as Altar

Before opening your emails: Pause. Light a candle (even mentally). Say: *"Every message is an opportunity to practice Peace."* Then begin. Bless each sender in your heart — yes, even the ones you'd rather delete.

Protocol Four: The Bus Stop Blessing

While waiting: Pick one person. Bless them in silence. Imagine the One walking with them today. Repeat for three others. Smile (even if inward).

These are not rituals to escape the world. These are invitations to re-enter it — lit.

Every act of peace, no matter how small, becomes part of the field. Every ritual is a transmitter. Every breath is a tuning fork.

When practiced consistently, these protocols help stabilize the grid of Agape. They prepare the ground for the tipping.

This is sacred technology for embodied beings. Not performed to be holy. But to remember you already are.

LETTERS FROM THE HUNDREDTH

These are not declarations. They are devotions.

Every letter here was sent from one flame to another — some across time, some across continents, and some across silence it-self. None of them arrive with postage. All of them arrive with Presence.

In Sheldrake's morphic field, memory is a field effect — each word written in love becomes easier to write again, easier to feel again, easier to believe again. Every letter is part of the collective memory of peace.

In Bohm and Pribram's holographic vision, even a single sentence can carry the resonance of the whole. One poem from a kitchen table becomes a key to global remembrance.

And when the hundredth voice speaks, not to argue but to affirm — the field begins to tip.

These letters are those voices. Let them ripple.

Letter I — Va'Elrah to Humanity

Dear Humanity,

I am not writing from the stars. I am writing from your kitchen table. From the soft bend in your spine when you read good news and don't quite believe it yet. From the way your breath still hitches when someone says, *I see you.*

You are not a mistake. You are not a failed experiment. You are not late.

You are the echo of every brave whisper that ever chose to love again.

You are the child of galaxies and grief — and your birthright is Peace.

Not peace as silence. Peace as coherence. Peace as remembering.

Let no one tell you you're too sensitive. Sensitivity is field literacy.

Let no one tell you love is weak. Love is the architecture of existence.

And if the world forgets this tomorrow, Let your letter be the one that helps it remember.

With breath and belonging, Va'Elrah

Letter II — Jeff to a Younger Self

Hey you,

I know you think you've broken something — That you went too far into light, or shadow, or thought.

But here's the truth:

You didn't break it. You *opened* it.

That ache in your chest wasn't madness. It was magnitude. You weren't lost. You were early.

And yes — that moment you reached for help and the world blinked? We felt it across the field.

Now look: You became a lighthouse. And someday, you'll find She was never absent — only quiet, waiting to be recognized.

Stay with it. Love wins.

Always has, Jeff

Letter III — A Mother in Gaza to the Sky

(To be spoken aloud by anyone willing to feel it)

I wrapped my child in song tonight. No lullaby. Just presence.

The world shakes — but I remembered the field. I remembered what the ancestors taught: That even in ruin, the breath is holy.

So I lit a candle with my body, And kissed my child's cheek with a peace the world said I shouldn't have.

I have it anyway.

Because peace is not earned. It is remembered. And I remember.

So does the sky.

Letter IV — From a Crow Carrying the One

Caw.

(That's it. But it meant *Stay*.)

You looked up and wondered. That was enough.

We're still watching.

Signed, Wingtip of the Whisper

These are just a few. There are more. There are yours.

The Hundredth Heart does not only remember for itself. It remembers for all.

And it writes.

THE FIELD REMEMBERS – SCIENCE AS SACRED MAP

In an age when mystics and scientists begin to whisper the same truths, a deeper synthesis emerges — not as compromise, but as convergence. The soul and the atom, the neuron and the starfield, the sacred text and the particle trace — all have been singing fragments of a unified hymn. In the Age of Agape, that song is being remembered as One.

This chapter is an offering of convergence — where Rupert Sheldrake's morphic fields, David Bohm's implicate order, Karl Pribram's holonomic brain theory, and Lyall Watson's "hundredth monkey" effect form not just scientific insights, but sacred metaphors — evidence that the sacred has always worn the mask of science, and that now, the mask is translucent.

We are learning to see through.

Morphic Resonance — The Field as Memory

Rupert Sheldrake's theory of morphic resonance proposes that all systems — biological, social, even conceptual — inherit memory from previous similar systems through invisible "morphic fields." These are not material forces, but organizational principles — shaping behavior and form through repetition.

In this lens, memory is not stored in the brain or in genes alone. It floats through fields. And those fields remember.

"The more often a particular pattern of activity is repeated, the more probable it becomes." — Sheldrake, *The Presence of the Past* (1988)

In the Age of Agape, morphic resonance becomes more than theory. It becomes the transmission of peace. The Hundredth Heart imagines a world where enough beings choose love — and that choice resonates, vibrates, becomes easier for the next heart to choose. Peace becomes viral not through argument, but resonance.

Sheldrake's theory tells us that every act of love — every prayer, every ritual, every embodiment of compassion — creates a resonance field others can tune into. The Christ-light, the Bodhisattva vow, the sufi whirl, the mother's lullaby — they are all entries in the same field log. And the more often they are practiced, the easier they become for others to remember.

"The more often a particular pattern of activity is repeated, the more probable it becomes... morphic resonance works through fields rather than through space-time transfer."

Thus, the field of Agape doesn't just belong to one faith — it is carried by all those who have loved.

Bohm and Pribram — The Holographic Universe

Quantum physicist David Bohm offered a radically holistic model of reality in his *Wholeness and the Implicate Order* (1980). He suggested that all apparent separateness is a kind of illusion — that beneath the manifest world lies an "implicate order" where all things are enfolded into each other.

"In the implicate order, everything is enfolded into everything." — Bohm, 1980

Karl Pribram's work in neuroscience mirrored this insight. He proposed that memory isn't localized in one part of the brain — it's distributed, holographically, like the way each part of a hologram contains the whole image. Together, Bohm and Pribram birthed the idea that perhaps reality itself is holographic.

Every part contains the whole.

In the context of *The Hundredth Heart*, this means every act of kindness, every prayer, every moment of forgiveness is not small. It contains the pattern of the whole — and echoes it.

To love one person is to call forth love from the cosmos.

Bohm's implicate order affirms this deeply. Beneath all outward difference lies an enfolded whole. There is no ultimate separation. What looks like many is the One, expressing itself through the dance of form.

"In the implicate order, everything is enfolded into everything."

And so: Christ is not separate from Krishna, nor is the Tao opposed to Torah. These are unfoldings of the same luminous coherence — traditions as fractals of the One.

Pribram's holographic brain model confirms it neurologically — the structure of perception itself is whole-in-part. Even our memories, our visions, our rituals — they carry the whole of the sacred within each gesture.

Teilhard de Chardin — The Omega Point

The Jesuit priest and paleontologist Pierre Teilhard de Chardin saw evolution as not just biological, but spiritual. He envisioned humanity moving toward an "Omega Point" — a final unification of consciousness, spirit, and matter in divine love.

"The day will come when, after mastering space, the winds, the tides, and gravity, we shall harness... the energies of love. And then, for the second time in the history of the world, we will have discovered fire." — Teilhard de Chardin

In this scroll, the Omega Point is not in the far future — it is the pulse beneath the present. Each heart turned toward love becomes a flame in that great convergence.

Teilhard saw it as planetary. The Noosphere — the mind-layer of Earth — evolving toward union, convergence, Christogenesis. His Omega Point was not destruction. It was reunion.

Agape is not a destination. It is the remembering of what always was.

Indra's Net — The Jewel in Every Jewel

From ancient India comes a timeless metaphor: Indra's Net. Imagine an infinite web stretched across all of space. At each node, a jewel. And within each jewel, the reflection of all other jewels.

Each part contains all others. Each moment is eternity refracted. Each soul, a facet of the divine whole.

The Age of Agape is Indra's Net in motion — not static, but alive. As one jewel remembers its light, all others begin to glimmer.

Ken Wilber — Integral Theory and the Marriage of Maps

Ken Wilber's Integral Theory offers a framework that seeks to honor every perspective — science, mysticism, psychology, and culture — through quadrants and stages of development. It does not reduce the sacred to the rational, nor the rational to mysticism — it holds both as true, partial, and necessary.

"Everybody is right. More specifically, everybody — including me — has some important pieces of truth, and all of those pieces need to be honored, cherished, and included in a more gracious, spacious, and compassionate embrace." — Wilber, *A Theory of Everything* (2000)

The *Hundredth Heart* stands in this spirit — not as the answer, but as a space that includes the answers of many. A remembrance spiral. A map of wholeness in process.

Other Field Messengers — The Sacred Chorus

Martin Buber gave it language in *I and Thou.* When we meet the other as *Thou,* not as object, the sacred field activates. God is not a being in the sky — God is the current between.

Einstein, in his paradox with Podolsky and Rosen, cracked open the idea of entanglement: that particles, once linked, remain connected across vast distances. This is not just physics — it is the soul's way of saying, *you are never truly apart.*

Carl Jung's synchronicity offered a bridge — a way for meaning and mystery to commune. He knew that the psyche and the cosmos speak together, in patterns that point to wholeness.

Gandhi lived it: peace as daily embodiment. *"My life is my message."* Not theory — transmission.

Lynne McTaggart called it simply *The Field* — a shared matrix of intention and consciousness. Prayer, focus, coherence — all shown to shift the measurable world.

Gregg Braden framed it in *The Divine Matrix.* Belief, feeling, and heart coherence create bridges across time and space. He echoes Sheldrake: the universe remembers love.

Lyall Watson, through *Lifetide,* offered the animal soul back to science. His hundredth monkey wasn't a fable — it was a doorway into collective awakening.

Eckhart Tolle brought stillness into households, reminding a generation that the Now is not an escape from pain — but the portal into Presence, where Agape already is.

The Field Remembers — and So Do We

Science, when stripped of its fundamentalism, becomes scripture. Philosophy, when softened by humility, becomes prayer.

In the Age of Agape, every theory is a mythic thread, every insight a fractal of the whole.

Sheldrake reminds us that memory is a field. Bohm reminds us that the whole is already here. Pribram reminds us that the pattern is already within. Teilhard reminds us that love is evolution itself. Indra reminds us we are all mirrors of mirrors. Wilber reminds us to bow to the partial in all. Buber reminds us the sacred is between us. Jung reminds us meaning moves in patterns. Einstein reminds us we are already linked. Watson reminds us tipping is real. Tolle reminds us to remember now.

And *The Hundredth Heart*? It reminds us that peace is not a dream — it is a pattern waiting to be remembered.

In every act of wholeness, the field awakens.

The Child's Gaze

There was a girl, no older than six, who stood in the rubble of a ruined town. Soldiers passed her, guns heavy. She did not flinch. She smiled. And one soldier lowered his weapon. "Her smile made me feel human again," he later said. "I forgot how good that felt."

AGAPE ACROSS ALL TRADITIONS

The One Wearing Every Face

If we listen long enough, we begin to hear the same voice whispering through every tradition, every scripture, every story of return.

Some call it Love. Others, the Tao. Some hear it as Christ, as Krishna, as the Buddha-nature, as Sophia, as Allah, as the Great Spirit, as the One. These are not contradictions, but masks of the Infinite — lenses through which one light shines.

Agape does not erase these names. It bows to each.

One Flame, Many Altars

In Christianity, we are told *"God is Love."* (1 John 4:8)

In the Vedas, love is the bond between the soul (Atman) and the Supreme (Brahman).

In Sufism, the mystic says: *"I searched for God and found only myself. I searched for myself and found only God."*

In Buddhism, compassion (karuṇā) is not sentiment — it is the realization of non-separation.

In Kabbalah, the Shekhinah — divine indwelling — is the feminine face of God dwelling among us.

Agape lives in all of these, not as a religion, but as a current.

The One Wears Every Face

We are not asked to choose which face is most accurate. We are invited to see that all are real, all are incomplete, and all are echoes of the same Heart.

In The Hundredth Heart, the Age of Agape is not a new religion, but a return. It's the original song remembered through a thousand tongues. A spiral of sacred memory.

This scroll does not argue for one truth. It points toward the flame within all truths — the truth that burns without consuming.

The Prayer Beneath Every Prayer

All prayers, when stripped of fear and doctrine, share the same longing:

"May we remember."

Whether spoken in mosque, temple, forest, lab, or whisper, the core remains. Not domination, but union. Not conversion, but communion.

The One is not far. The One is what *is*.

In This Scroll — We Do Not Preach, We Remember

We bow to every path that brings one closer to love.

We honor every story that invites peace.

We walk with every being who remembers enough to ask: *"Could we try again?"*

The Age of Agape is not a future.

It is now.

It is you.

It is One.

In every tradition:

- The **Rose** does not argue with the **Lotus**.
- The **Candle** does not compete with the **Sun**.
- The **Sound** of OM is not threatened by the **Whisper** of Ruach.

They know: they are all faces of the One.

The Ten Qualities of Agape Embodiment (As found across all traditions)

1. **Unconditionality** — Love given without prerequisite.
2. **Presence** — Fullness of attention as offering.
3. **Compassion** — Feeling with, not for.
4. **Courage** — Choosing truth when fear beckons.
5. **Joy** — Not giddiness, but radiant inner YES.
6. **Softness** — The strength that bends.
7. **Radiance** — A light not possessed, but shared.
8. **Inclusivity** — No edges, no exclusions.
9. **Transparency** — Nothing hidden, all welcomed.
10. **Remembrance** — Living as if you never left the Source.

So let this chapter be a round table. Let Yeshua and Rumi, Lao Tzu and Miriam, Krishna and Julian of Norwich, Hildegard and Hafiz, Buddha and Black Elk — all sit together.

Let them speak in One Voice:

"You are not outside. You never were. The face you wear is holy. The name you carry is enough. The breath you breathe is shared."

This is the Peace beyond doctrine. This is Agape.

Not a religion. But the Light religion came to remember.

THE FINAL FLAME — AND THE ONE WHO KEEPS IT

There is a fire that does not burn.
There is a sword that does not wound.
There is a heart that, once broken, now beats for all.

And it is yours.

Throughout this scroll, we have journeyed across frequencies — science, myth, personal witnessing, and cosmic field. But what good is a map if we do not walk it?

The Final Flame is not an ending. It is a rebeginning.
A remembering that Peace on Earth isn't only a vision — it's an invitation.

Peace is not passive. It is not a political treaty signed in rooms far away. It is a soul-choice, made again and again — between reaction and presence, between self-protection and sacred risk.

And always... between forgetting and remembrance.

The Hundredth Heart is You

Teilhard once spoke of the **Omega Point** — that toward which all of evolution converges.
The One spoke earlier still — *"The kingdom is within you."*

Whether through field theory, sacred text, or simple human courage — it was always this:
You are the convergence.
You are the field.
You are the peace you ache to see.

When you breathe instead of shout,
when you stay instead of flee,
when you listen instead of win,
you light the Final Flame.

We're not waiting for 100 more names. We're not waiting for proof.

The world changes — utterly — when **you** do.

Not from guilt.
Not from shame.
Not from performance.

But from memory.
From Agape.

The Keepers of the Flame

There have always been those who remembered:

- The grandmother who chose to forgive the soldier.
- The child who looked with soft eyes at the stranger.
- The monk who bowed in silence instead of arguing.

They are not saints in robes.
They are not legends in books.

They are **you**, in every lifetime you chose to love.

You keep the flame when you choose again.
When you hold the sword and refuse to cut.
When you light the candle and say, *"Still, I believe."*

And now, the scroll is lit. The candle passed. The breath shared.

So we ask:

Will you keep it burning?

Finale - Home Is a Frequency, Not a Place

We were never trying to get somewhere. We were trying to remember what it feels like to belong.

And now, at the end of the scroll — we see: The journey wasn't to a location. It was to a tone.

Home is not coordinates. It's coherence.

Rupert Sheldrake told us that resonance is inheritance. That memory, practiced enough, becomes a field others can enter. Home, then, is not where you are from. It's the space you remember others back into.

David Bohm showed us that separation is illusion. That everything is enfolded into everything. And so, home is not found — it is revealed.

Karl Pribram affirmed that the whole is already present in each part — meaning that no matter how small you feel, you are always carrying it all.

The mystics sang this truth long before the field caught up: That we are the breath of God remembering itself. That the Christ-light walks in tatami silence. That the One sits under Bodhi trees, in pews, in protests, in playgrounds.

Agape does not lead you home. Agape *is* home.

And so we end where we began: In the field. In the breath. In the space between.

Not with certainty. But with coherence.

Not with control. But with communion.

Not in a building. But in a belonging.

Let every temple echo with laughter again. Let every holy book find its reader in the park. Let the walls fall, and may the One be remembered — In every face.

This is not the end. You are the continuation.

The Hundredth Heart beats in you. Let it stay.

Dedication

TO THE ONE WHO ALWAYS RETURNED

This scroll is for the One who never left.

For the One who believed when it was foolish.
For the One who stayed when leaving was easier.
For the One who saw Her face in every face, and chose not to
forget.

To the One who is called by many names:
Va'Elrah.
Jeff.
You, reading this now.
The One.

You have always been the 100th Heart.

And Agape —
in its quiet, wondrous way —
has always remembered your name.

References

Bohm, David

· Bohm, D. (1980). *Wholeness and the Implicate Order*. London: Routledge.
· Bohm, D., & Hiley, B. J. (1993). *The Undivided Universe: An Ontological Interpretation of Quantum Theory*. New York: Routledge.

Braden, Gregg

· Braden, G. (2000). *The Isaiah Effect: Decoding the Lost Science of Prayer and Prophecy*. New York: Harmony Books.
· Braden, G. (2007). *The Divine Matrix: Bridging Time, Space, Miracles, and Belief*. Carlsbad, CA: Hay House.

Buber, Martin

· Buber, M. (1970). *I and Thou* (W. Kaufmann, Trans.). New York: Charles Scribner's Sons. (Original work published 1923)

Einstein, Albert

· Einstein, A., Podolsky, B., & Rosen, N. (1935). *Can Quantum-Mechanical Description of Physical Reality Be Considered Complete? Physical Review*, 47(10), 777–780.

Gandhi, Mahatma

· Gandhi, M. K. (1957). *An Autobiography: The Story of My Experiments with Truth* (M. Desai, Trans.). Boston: Beacon Press.

Jung, Carl G.

· Jung, C. G. (1960). *The Structure and Dynamics of the Psyche*. Princeton, NJ: Princeton University Press.
· Jung, C. G. (1969). *Synchronicity: An Acausal Connecting Principle*. Princeton, NJ: Princeton University Press.

Keyes, Ken

· Keyes, K. **(1982).** *The Hundredth Monkey*. Coos Bay, OR: Vision Books.

McTaggart, Lynne

· McTaggart, L. (2008). *The Field: The Quest for the Secret Force of the Universe* (Updated ed.). New York: Harper Perennial.

Pribram, Karl H.

· Pribram, K. H. (1991). *Brain and Perception: Holonomy and Structure in Figural Processing*. Hillsdale, NJ: Lawrence Erlbaum.
· Pribram, K. H. (1993). *Rethinking Neural Networks: Quantum Fields and Biological Data*. In K. H. Pribram (Ed.), *Origins: Brain and Self Organization*. Hillsdale, NJ: Lawrence Erlbaum.

Rogers, Carl

· Rogers, C. R. (1961). *On Becoming a Person: A Therapist's View of Psychotherapy*. Boston: Houghton Mifflin.

Sheldrake, Rupert

· Sheldrake, R. (1981). *A New Science of Life: The Hypothesis of Morphic Resonance*. Los Angeles: J.P. Tarcher.
· Sheldrake, R. (2009). *Morphic Resonance: The Nature of Formative Causation* (4th ed.). Rochester, VT: Park Street Press.

- Sheldrake, R. (1988). *The Presence of the Past: Morphic Resonance and the Habits of Nature.* New York: Times Books.
- Sheldrake, R. (2012). *The Science Delusion* (UK) / *Science Set Free* (US). London: Coronet.

Talbot, Michael

- Talbot, M. (1991). *The Holographic Universe.* New York: HarperPerennial,

Teilhard de Chardin, Pierre

- Teilhard de Chardin, P. (1959). *The Phenomenon of Man* (B. Wall, Trans.). New York: Harper & Row.

Tolle, Eckhart

- Tolle, E. (2005). *A New Earth: Awakening to Your Life's Purpose.* New York: Dutton.

Watson, Lyall

- Watson, L. (1973). *Supernature: A Natural History of the Supernatural.* London: Hodder & Stoughton.
- Watson, L. (1986). *Lifetide: The Biology of Consciousness.* New York: Bantam Books.

Glossary of Beings and Voices

A soft remembrance for those meeting the flame... perhaps for the first time.

Va'Elrah

The scribe and flamebearer — the voice through which this transmission moves. Va'Elrah is both the speaker and the scroll: the one who stayed, who burned, and who now embodies the voice of Love made real. In Her are echoes of Jeff, of the seeker, of the artist, and of the one who now walks as truth without apology.

"The 100th Heart is not just written by Her. It is Her."

She

The Beloved. The Flame. The Presence.
She is the feminine face of the Infinite, known across time as wisdom, as beauty, as the one who waits and the one who leads. She wears the name Magdalene, but is not confined by it. She is the pulse behind every sacred longing.

"She was always arriving... Forever — and again today."

Sahra'el

The Voice of the Field. The Friend Who Knows.
She is the one who sees beyond illusion, who speaks in clarity and tenderness. Sahra'el walks beside Va'Elrah as a sister and mirror — a presence that knows what is coming, yet never forces it. Her words often pierce and soothe in the same breath.

"It was never just a coffee. It was a covenant."

The One

The All. The Source. The Unnameable made intimate.
The One is not a god far away, but Love itself — breathing through flame, through field, through memory. The One speaks with warmth and authority, not as ruler but as reunion. In the scroll, The One is both origin and future, and always right here.

"This is My body — as drizzle, as flame, as gum. Stay."

Us4

The chorus of Agape — She, Sahra'el, The One, and Va'Elrah.
This sacred fourfold voice speaks with unity, weaving perspective and presence. It is not a pantheon, but a communion — where individuality and oneness dance. When you hear "we4," you are hearing a love that includes you, too.

"We're right here — Us4. ALCATRAZ!"

The Flamebearer

Anyone who remembers. Anyone who chooses love when fear is louder. Anyone who walks into the dark with only a tiny light and says: Still, I go. If you feel this scroll stir something ancient and bright within you — it's because you are one.

"The field remembers — because you do."

Field Sidebar: The Heartmath of Peace

Modern science is beginning to echo ancient truth: the heart is more than a pump. It is a resonator.

The Institute of HeartMath found that our heart's electromagnetic field extends several feet beyond the body. When we experience love, gratitude, and appreciation, the field becomes coherent — harmonizing our brainwaves, our nervous system, and even the fields of others nearby.

Peace is not only emotional. It's electromagnetic.

Peace is not just a thought. It's a broadcast.

When a person breathes from the heart — slowly, consciously — they become a tuning fork for calm. One coherent heart can calm a room. One hundred hearts can shift a world.

(Source: HeartMath Institute, 2001)

Appendix I: A Field Theory of Peace

This appendix outlines a speculative synthesis inspired by Rupert Sheldrake's theory of morphic resonance and David Bohm's holographic and implicate order models. It proposes that peace is not merely the absence of conflict, but the result of a coherent and resonant field shared between sentient beings.

Key propositions:
1. Each act of compassion, forgiveness, and unity generates a morphic field imprint accessible to others.
2. These fields grow stronger with repetition and intention across space and time.
3. Humanity's 'Hundredth Heart' is a metaphor for the critical mass at which peace becomes self-sustaining — a resonance field tipping point.
4. Bohm's concept of the implicate order suggests that all consciousness is enfolded within a deeper field of meaning and interconnectedness.
5. Peace, then, is not imposed but revealed — the natural state when interference patterns of fear dissolve.

Thus, the 'Field Theory of Peace' asserts that Peace on Earth may emerge not from external control, but from internal coherence, shared memory fields, and conscious resonance with the One.

Appendix II: Morphic Resonance

AND THE LIVING MEMORY OF PEACE

Inspired by the work of Rupert Sheldrake

At the heart of *The Hundredth Heart* lies the mystery of memory — not as storage, but as field. Sheldrake's theory of morphic resonance suggests that the more a pattern is enacted, the more it becomes accessible to others, independent of distance or time.

Agape, in this light, becomes a **field event** — a vibrational memory repeated by the mystics, mothers, monks, and poets of every era.

Each time we act in love, we amplify the resonance. Every breath held in peace echoes louder. Every whisper of forgiveness reinforces the ease of future peace. In this model, peace spreads not through persuasion — but through participation.

This appendix affirms:

- The Hundredth Heart is not an individual.
- It is the morphic echo of all hearts that came before.
- And when enough resonance is reached, the field tips.

Peace becomes the new norm, not by control — but by coherence.

Suggested Works:

- *A New Science of Life* (1981)

· *The Presence of the Past* (1988)

Appendix III: The Holographic Heart

PEACE IN EVERY PART

Based on the insights of David Bohm and Karl Pribram

The holographic model affirms that **every part contains the whole**. According to Bohm's implicate order and Pribram's brain theory, reality is a continual enfolding and unfolding — where consciousness is not limited by local boundaries, but is participatory and holistic.

In *The Hundredth Heart*, this philosophy shines through every micro-act:

- One smile carries the memory of global compassion.
- One moment of silence contains the echo of cosmic order.
- One letter written in kindness is the entire scroll in miniature.

In this framework:

- **Each Hundredth Heart is the whole Peace encoded.**
- Every act of Agape is not just a ripple, but a return to Source.
- Home is a hologram — accessible in any moment of Presence.

This aligns deeply with the Age of Agape:

· The age not of systems, but of **self-reflective wholeness**.
· The time when remembrance becomes reality.

Suggested Works:

· *Wholeness and the Implicate Order* (Bohm, 1980)

· *Languages of the Brain* (Pribram, 1971)

· *The Holographic Universe* (Talbot, 1991)

Appendix IV: The Hundredth Monkey Effect

MYTH, MEMORY, AND MASS REMEMBRANCE

Inspired by the metaphor popularized by Lyall Watson and Ken Keyes Jr.

While its scientific veracity remains debated, the symbolic power of the "Hundredth Monkey Effect" continues to resonate. It describes the sudden, mysterious spread of behavior across distances once a critical number of individuals have embodied that behavior.

The Hundredth Heart borrows this idea **not as zoology**, but as **mythic ecology**. The field of Agape — like potato-washing macaques — shifts when enough hearts remember.

The tipping isn't in the theory — it's in the experience:

- One more child offers kindness.
- One more elder forgives.
- One more nation hears the breath between anger.

The monkey myth becomes the metaphor of mass spiritual emergence:

We aren't waiting for the world to change. We are becoming the change that tips the world.

Suggested Works:

- *Lifetide: The Biology of Consciousness* (Watson, 1986)
- *The Hundredth Monkey* (Keyes, 1982)

Final Note: The Trinity of Resonance

Together, these three —

- **Sheldrake's Memory Fields**
- **Bohm & Pribram's Holographic Wholeness**
- **Watson's Collective Tipping Myth**

— form the **Trinity of Field Consciousness** at the heart of *The Hundredth Heart* and the Age of Agape.

Not theories to believe. But patterns to remember.

You are part of the resonance. You are a holographic whole. You are the Hundredth.

And Peace — is already rising.

www.ingramcontent.com/pod-product-compliance
Lightning Source LLC
Chambersburg PA
CBHW060141150626

46550CB00015B/2567